# ASPECTS

## OF

# DOCTOR JOHNSON

T0382302

# ASPECTS
## OF
# DOCTOR JOHNSON

*By*

E. S. ROSCOE

CAMBRIDGE

*At the University Press*

1928

*To*

MY FRIENDS & FELLOW MEMBERS
*Past and Present*
OF THE
JOHNSON CLUB

# CAMBRIDGE
## UNIVERSITY PRESS

University Printing House, Cambridge CB2 8BS, United Kingdom

Cambridge University Press is part of the University of Cambridge.

It furthers the University's mission by disseminating knowledge in the pursuit of education, learning and research at the highest international levels of excellence.

www.cambridge.org
Information on this title: www.cambridge.org/9781316509616

© Cambridge University Press 1928

First published 1928
First paperback edition 2015

*A catalogue record for this publication is available from the British Library*

ISBN 978-1-316-50961-6 Paperback

# PREFATORY NOTE

THE studies contained in the following pages are united by a common motive—the illustration and illumination of the character of Dr Johnson. In spite of the great revival of interest in the life and work of Johnson during the present century, it may be doubted whether his character is by any means fully understood. It is hoped that these studies may, in some measure, assist in a larger appreciation of his remarkable personality.

With the exception of those on Johnson and Selden and on Johnson's Religion, these papers have already been printed in periodicals and I have to thank the proprietors of the *Cornhill Magazine*, the *National Review* and the *North American Review* for their courteous permission to reprint.

To my friend Mr S. C. Roberts I am very much indebted for his kind interest in this book during its progress through the press.

E. S. R.

*March 1928*

# CONTENTS

## § I

## JOHNSON'S CHARACTER

*The Art of Living*
*Johnson and the Law*
*Johnson's Religion*

# THE ART OF LIVING

LISTENING once to the annual Johnson sermon in Lichfield Cathedral it occurred to me that such a service would have been both impossible and inappropriate if Johnson were considered merely as an eminent man of letters. The Doctor once used the expression "the art of living", and it seemed clear that the chief reason of this celebration in Lichfield Cathedral of Johnson's birth was the fact that he was pre-eminently a teacher, to use his own words, of the art of living.

For a teacher of the conduct of life, Johnson had every requisite qualification. A scholar of immense, if desultory, scope of reading in ancient and modern authors, with a very retentive memory, he was full of experience gained from many books in several languages and of all times, and he valued reading for this reason: "What should books teach", he said, "but the art of living?" To this essential qualification of literary experience, Johnson added experience obtained from close personal association with eminent men like Burke, Fox, Reynolds, Goldsmith, and Stowell. He was familiar with nearly every class, both social and political, and he cultivated friendship with women not less than with men; he was a man of the world, in the best sense of the words. If we enumerate the great English figures of the eighteenth century, can we find another in whom were united in so especial and unusual degree the experiences which qualified him to be a teacher of the conduct of life?

But experience alone would not have been enough; it might have been only a dormant force. If, however, we analyse Johnson's famous sayings, it will be found that they have three predominant characteristics: sincerity, lucidity, and vigour. These qualities are visible in his

writings, as much as in his talk, and each
was essential for the effective, one may
even say the popular, presentation of
moral truths. In fact, he sometimes put
them so concisely and clearly that they
seem almost trite maxims. "He who
chuses earliest, chuses best", is advice in
a form which might fitly be hung in any
class-room. Again, "It is no less dan-
gerous for any man to . . . fancy that he
is born to be illustrious without labour,
than to omit the cares of husbandry, and
to expect from his ground the blossoms
of Arabia", is a passage from a paper in
the *Rambler*. Here is a platitude pictur-
esquely dressed, for Johnson possessed
the gift of extracting principles from details, and of stating them not merely as
maxims, but as living truths. Take as an
example, from another paper in the
*Rambler*, this suggestive sentence: "There
is nothing more unsuitable to the nature
of man in any calamity than rage and
turbulence . . . which are at least always
offensive and incline others rather to hate

and despise than to pity and assist us ".
Burke applied the same power, but more
impressively, to politics, as for example in
the sentence: "A nation is not governed
which is perpetually to be conquered".
In the sphere of law the same faculty was
remarkable alike in Mansfield and Stowell.
The one showed it in his illuminating
judgments on commercial law, the other
in the sonorous sentences with which he
embellished his decisions on maritime
and prize law.

The next point to be noted is that
Johnson's teaching of the art of living
was spontaneous and unpremeditated.
For example, before he began to write
his essays in the *Rambler*, he made a
business-like arrangement for payment of
two guineas a paper, which amounted to
an income of four guineas a week, or
more than £200 a year, as long as the
*Rambler* continued to be published. The
primary object of this project was to
please his readers so that the periodical
might obtain a considerable circulation.

He proposed "to endeavour the entertainment of [his] countrymen by a short
essay on Tuesday and Saturday". Entertainment may possibly be regarded as in-
cluding education, but be that as it may,
Johnson's intention was, first of all, to
interest and please his readers. But before he began his work he composed the
remarkable and touching *Prayer on the
Rambler*, in which he prays to God that
he "may promote Thy glory and the
salvation both of myself and others".
The promotion of salvation, which need
not be regarded in a narrow, religious
light, is the business of a teacher of the
art of living, and Johnson's mind, when
he composed this prayer, had begun to
regard his journal as a means towards the
moral guidance of his readers, which, in
fact, it became. "Of his virtues", wrote
Sir Joshua Reynolds, "the most dis-
tinguished was his love of truth". The
combination of a love of truth and a
vigorous mind, "a strong mind operating
upon life", as Johnson said of Bacon,

caused him in his writings and in his conversation to apply for the benefit of others those precepts which he had himself formulated for his own good. The teacher was stronger than either the man of business who had to earn his livelihood or the man of letters who took pleasure in literary expression; and the same qualities were as obvious in much of his conversation as in much of his written work. While he loved sociable talk and lively argument, he could hardly converse for any length of time or on any serious subject before he became, momentarily it might be, a teacher. But, as a man of the world, he gave sound advice on the art of living at the fitting moment and in an acceptable form. "Do not", said the Doctor, when Boswell was talking of his approaching marriage, "expect more from life than life will afford". And, when on the death of his father, Boswell became owner of the Auchinleck property, he gave him much excellent advice. "Begin your new course of life", he wrote, "with the least show and the least expense possible: you may at pleasure increase both but you cannot easily diminish them. Do not think your estate your own, while any man can call upon you for money, which you cannot pay; therefore begin with timorous parsimony. Let it be your first care not to be in any man's debt". When he took the trouble to write, in 1763, to George Strahan, then a boy at school, with hints upon study, he could not refrain in each letter from urging him to be diligent—"Any method will do, if there be but diligence". Yet Johnson never posed as a superior person, and while his teaching was spontaneous and unpremeditated, it was never emotional; it always bears the stamp of the common sense which was a characteristic of himself, of his age, and of the English people.

The hardships and difficulties of Johnson's early and middle years and his weak health are well known. These could not fail to influence unconsciously his views of life from day to day. When we bear in mind further that at all times he was a realist, that he had no delusions about the course of human life, that he never allowed imagination to vary its appearance or to obscure its actual state, it is not surprising that he dwelt too often, perhaps, on the gloomier aspects of existence.

Pour forth thy fervours for a healthful mind,
Obedient passions and a will resigned,

is advice based on a gloomy view of the human scene, as gloomy as that of Thomas Hardy. *The Vanity of Human Wishes* is, in fact, from beginning to end, an exhortation to be under no illusions, as sound advice on the art of living as can be given by any teacher. But after all, *The Vanity of Human Wishes* and *Rasselas* contain but half the truth; human life is not altogether so hopeless as would be surmised from the poem. It has sunnier aspects, and Johnson was too clear-sighted not to perceive and appreciate them. Further, he tried to show how these could be obtained and to demonstrate the satisfaction which resulted from their enjoyment. It would not be easy to find a passage in greater contrast to *The Vanity of Human Wishes* than the paper in the *Rambler* on "Spring". Its conclusion is as encouraging as the poem is depressing:

He that enlarges his curiosity after the works of nature demonstrably multiplies the inlets to happiness; and, therefore, the younger part of my readers, to whom I dedicate this vernal speculation, must excuse me for calling upon them to make use at once of the spring of year, and the spring of life; to acquire, while their minds may yet be impressed with new images, a love of innocent pleasures, and an ardour for useful knowledge; and to remember that a blighted spring makes a barren year, and that the vernal flowers, however beautiful and gay, are only intended by nature as preparatives to autumnal fruits.

This advice is not only sound, but is also a recognition of the existence of happiness in human life side by side with the vanity of many human aspirations. If it be a truism, it is expressed in a form which attracts, and advice is palatable as much by virtue of the way in which it is offered as from its inherent truth. Johnson's mind was too sane to dwell constantly only on one aspect of life. It would scarcely be possible to find a better instance of this, and of the sanity of his teaching, than the saying that men should keep their friendships in constant repair, so opposed, for example, to the mournful regret of *In Memoriam* and even the note of irremediable personal loss in *Lycidas* and in Shelley's *Adonais*.

Hawthorne, in one of his literary pieces which were collected in *Our Old Home*, complains that Johnson as a moralist, by which he means a teacher, did not go below the surface of things. Hawthorne's antagonism, for it almost amounts to that, was the result of temperamental differences. Johnson's bluntness and directness were distasteful to the susceptible and imaginative mind of the author of *The Scarlet Letter* and of *The Marble Faun*. To Johnson, the surface of things,

and it was a pretty large surface, was sufficient because he was averse from speculation and accepted religion, law, and the
English Constitution as he found them.
He stood up for broad, general truths
and he struck at the leading faults of the
common mass of humanity. He did not
trouble himself to study and discover
either the gifts or the weaknesses of ex-
ceptional character or to feel the delicate
filaments of emotional constitutions. It
followed that, whether he was regarding
merits or faults, he treated them as existing and did not attempt to seek out the
causes of their existence.

This obvious limitation, characteristic
of much of the thought of the eighteenth
century, has one noticeable result: it gives
permanence to Johnson's teaching. For
this teaching dealt with subjects, motives,
and actions which concern the majority
of mankind as it is to-day and as it will
be to-morrow. No one, says Professor
Trevelyan, ever discussed the problem of
conduct so well as Johnson in any age or

country "from the point of view of the plain man's thoughts and instincts". Advice such as Johnson gives will always be valuable and will outlive many passing theories and speculations. It appeals directly and forcibly to the ordinary man, to his strength and his weakness, but especially to his courage. "The business of life", he wrote to a friend sorrowing for the death of his mother, "summons us away from useless grief and calls us to the exercise of those virtues of which we are lamenting our deprivation". Self-reliance is a cardinal virtue and so he urges everyone to be the master of his own fate:

How small of all that human hearts endure,
That part which laws or kings can cause or cure.

To what extent did Johnson influence his contemporaries and posterity? A satisfactory answer is impossible, because Johnson was concerned with the ordinary life of ordinary people, and he was not advocating a particular doctrine—he was not a Wesley or a Savonarola. If one judges from the consensus of opinion among those who associated with him, one may be assured that many men and women of his own time, at any rate, were the better for his teaching.

Johnson's influence waned after his death, but there is evidence that the present generation has more appreciation of his work than had their immediate forefathers; and it may be that his realism, sincerity, and intellectual honesty are appreciated by those who have passed through the period of the Great War. Whether that be so or not, Johnson's striking individualism and his appeal to everyone to work out his own salvation by his own exertions, mental and physical, were never more valuable than they are to-day. "No man", said Sir Joshua Reynolds, who was a very acute observer of the contemporary scene, "had like him the faculty of teaching inferior minds the art of thinking", and not less, to use Johnson's own expression, "the art of living".

# JOHNSON AND THE LAW

"Sir," said Doctor Johnson, "it would have been better that I had been of a profession. I ought to have been a lawyer".

When people speak of the law they commonly mean not only jurisprudence and legal procedure, but the personal machinery of justice as well as the body of legal practitioners. It is in this sense that we must think of Johnson and the law.

Of his own fitness for the law Johnson had no doubt. To what extent was this view supported by others? A well-qualified observer, himself an eminent judge—Lord Stowell—said to Dr Johnson, "What a pity it is, sir, that you did not follow the profession of the law. You might have been Lord Chancellor". Here is a safe piece of flattery, but the statement was more than an idle compliment, for Stowell was too true a friend of Johnson, too shrewd an observer, to make a heedless remark on this subject. Johnson then, according to his own opinion, should have been a lawyer, which suggests that he had an accurate knowledge of his own abilities, as well as a clear perception of the necessary attributes of an advocate. Lord Stowell concurred in corroboration of Johnson's view; so also did Boswell and Dr Adams, the Master of Johnson's college.

How far were these opinions well founded? In the first place, Johnson pre-eminently possessed qualities required in a successful legal adviser and advocate —in particular, a robust and logical intellect, averse from subtlety. The late Lord Esher, at one time Master of the Rolls, used sometimes to say to a specially ingenious counsel, "Come, come, that is too fine". Such criticism would never have been applied to any argument of Johnson's. For Johnson had an inherent perception of the crucial fact in any set of circumstances, a quality capable of being cultivated by practice, but not a common quality either in lawyers or in laymen. Johnson moreover had a gift of clear expression and a copious and resonant vocabulary united with a capacity of statement in popular and forcible language. Perhaps an equally valuable quality was a power of a quickly-kindled argumentative warmth, which, had he been an advocate, would have enabled him to envelop the case of his clients with an atmosphere of fervid, if temporary, indignation. Again, the attractive common sense of his words was so willingly received by a hearer that the argument was apprehended without effort. Lord Elibank, who was a man of the world and a man of ability, once said to Boswell, "Whatever opinion Johnson maintains I will not say that he convinces me, but he never fails to show me that he has good reason for it". If we take Lord Elibank to represent an intelligent jury-man, or even an attentive judge, it is clear that Johnson as an advocate had gone a long way to win his case; and if we imagine the Doctor pitted against someone inferior to himself in the necessary qualities, we may well see him in full career as a successful barrister. Inherent perception and clear statement have been the basic causes of the success of every first-rate advocate. Often, they have been the main cause; and if hasty observers have been surprised at the success of a counsel lacking in showy attributes, it is because they have never appreciated the importance of these two qualities. On the other hand, eloquent advocates would never have attained their remarkable positions if they had had eloquence alone. They have all possessed an eye to main facts, varying no doubt in acuteness.

Johnson's habit of arguing was largely the spontaneous application of his special talents to intercourse in daily society. Why did he like Thurlow and call him a "fine fellow"? Because "he fairly puts his mind to yours". Because, in fact, he was a close and forcible arguer. Are we too imaginative if we surmise that the arguments between the man of letters and the lawyer were often on legal subjects? If they were, we have a glimpse of these verbal combats from what Cradock in his *Memoirs* says of the two disputants: "I was always more afraid of Johnson than of Thurlow; for though the latter was sometimes very rough and coarse, yet the decisive stroke of the former left a mortal wound behind it". In this passage the writer does not seem to describe an argument between the Doctor and the Judge, but rather one with himself, but the description fits an encounter in which the two remarkable minds were, in Johnson's phrase, "put" to each other.

If Johnson had gone to the bar and had spent his days in writing opinions and in arguing cases in court, or later in deciding them on the bench, it is possible that, having exhausted his powers in pro-fessional work, he would never have used them to delight or confound his friends. It was, however, the possession of these qualities which caused Johnson to enjoy the society of lawyers and the discussion of legal questions. On four occasions at least Johnson wrote a legal argument. The first was on a question of Scotch law as to the right of a person to intermeddle, without legal authority, with the effects of a deceased person. The legal point does not matter. Boswell says that he had exhausted all his own powers of reasoning in vain, and then come these significant words: "In order to assist me in my application to the court for a revision and alteration of the judgment, he dictated to me the following argument", which it is not necessary to quote here. Again, at a later date, when Boswell was counsel in an election petition he stated different points to Johnson, who, he says, "never failed to see them clearly and to give me some good hints". The arguments which Johnson wrote have been called by an unfriendly critic, a barrister, "very admirable and masterly and worthy the attention of the student". This is a valuable testimony, for not only is it the only good thing that the author can say for Johnson, but it is the evidence of a lawyer who, having studied Johnson's opinion from his own point of view, actually recommends to the student the legal arguments of the man of letters. These examples, and others which may be found in Boswell's *Life*, prove incontestably the legal character of Johnson's mind as well as his natural inclination to apply it to practical points of law. Indeed, is there a layman in existence who would, or could, sit down to dictate to a lawyer a legal argument of point and substance, unless he had a mind singularly adapted to the purpose and unless he had made a study of the principles of law and of legal decisions?

There can be little doubt that the law was in Johnson's mind for the best part of his life. In 1776, when he was sixty-seven, he said to Boswell, "I learnt what I know of law chiefly from Mr Ballow, a very able man. I learnt some too from Chambers, but was not so teachable then".

The first mention of Chambers, who succeeded Blackstone as Vinerian Professor at Oxford in 1762, is on 21 November 1754, when Johnson wrote to him at Oxford. In the summer of the same year he had visited Oxford "for the first time after quitting the University". On this visit Johnson, who was then forty-five, must have met Chambers. As to the time that the Doctor was intimate with Ballow we know nothing. He went to London in 1736: about 1739 he asked Dr Adams to consult Dr Smallbrooke, an advocate of Doctors' Commons, on his behalf, as to whether he could practise there without a Doctor's degree. It may have been at this time, when he found that he was ineligible as an advocate, that his thoughts turned to other branches of the law.

Whether he endeavoured to study law seriously with Ballow, who was a barrister of Lincoln's Inn and the author of a work on Equity, which at one time seems to have had great vogue in the chambers of Chancery barristers, we do not know. But it is quite clear that Johnson continued to discuss legal principles with his legal friends long after his first attempt to enter the legal profession; for his intimacy with Chambers began fifteen years after the application to Dr Smallbrooke, at a time when, as Johnson says, he was not so teachable, though evidently he was not too old to learn or to take an incessant interest in the law.

When he had reached the comparatively mature age of fifty-six, there occurred a curious incident—the writing (1765) of a Prayer before the study of the Law. Whether this prayer was written for himself, or for some young man about to begin a career as a lawyer, does not matter much. But it is a further testimony to the serious attention which Johnson gave to the law throughout his life, and his admirable statement of the moral and professional position of a lawyer as an advocate is as appropriate now as when it was uttered:

"Sir," he said, "a lawyer has no business with the justice or injustice of the cause he undertakes, unless his client asks his opinion, and then he is bound to give it honestly. The justice or injustice of the cause is to be decided by the judge. Consider, sir; what is the purpose of courts of justice? It is that every man may have his cause fairly tried by men appointed to try causes. A lawyer is not to tell what he knows to be a lie: he is not to produce what he knows to be a false deed; but he is not to usurp the province of the jury and of the judge, and determine what shall be the effect of evidence—what shall be the result of legal argument. As it rarely happens that a man is fit to plead his own cause, lawyers are a class of the community who, by study and experience, have acquired the art and power of arranging evidence, and of applying to the points at issue what the law has settled. A lawyer is to do for his client all that his client might fairly do for himself, if he could. If, by a superiority of attention, of knowledge, of skill, and a better method of communication, he has the advantage of his adversary, it is an advantage to which he is entitled. There must always be some advantage on one side or the other; and it is better that advantage should be had by talents than by chance. If lawyers were to undertake no causes till they were sure they were just, a man might be precluded altogether from a trial of his claim, though, were it judicially examined, it might be found a very just claim".

The rationale of advocacy has never been better expressed.

Is it not fair, then, to assert not only that Johnson's mind was that of a lawyer in the best sense, but that no man of letters ever gave so much attention to the subject of the law? English law, with its steady growth, its common sense, and its close connection with the life and temperament of the English people, was peculiarly attractive to him. This tendency would naturally make Johnson appreciate the society of lawyers; for he was not, as are most people, unless they happen to be litigants, averse from discussing with them the subject on which most of their lives was spent; on the other hand, the society of the lawyers with whom he foregathered must have increased his appreciation of law as well as of lawyers.

So far we have contemplated Johnson's character in relation to law and advocacy. But there is another point of view. Successful solicitors have owed their success to sagacity, that is, to an inherent perception of right action in practical affairs. This is by no means a common gift; it is a union of many qualities, but it springs in the main from a peculiar, instinctive perception. To advise successfully not only on technique but on conduct, whether in business or general affairs, requires a pre-eminent amount of sagacity. Johnson possessed this quality. One has only to be familiar with his essays in the *Rambler* to perceive how bountifully he was endowed with it. To Taine, and to others, these essays seemed dull reading. It is true that, like most essays, they contain com-

monplaces, but they also contain an un-
usually large store of wisdom applied to
ordinary human affairs. Here, again, is
a quality which, if Johnson had been an
attorney, would have made him a first-
rate adviser, equally at home in technical
and in general matters; nor can one
doubt that he would have been a most
successful member of this branch of the
profession.

Proximity has much to do with friendship. "The tide of life", the Doctor once
rather pathetically remarked, referring
to his first law teacher Ballow, "has
driven us different ways". And if it be
true that Johnson had a legal mind, the
fact that he lived within reach of the Inns
of Court and of Doctors' Commons
would naturally lead him to cultivate the
society of the lawyers who were his
neighbours.

For Johnson the members of the College of Advocates whose home was in
Doctors' Commons had a peculiar attrac-
tion. They were a singular body, half

academic and half legal, so that with them Johnson would have each side of their lives in common. Sir James Marriott, who preceded Lord Stowell as Judge of the Admiralty and Prize Court, was at the same time Master of Trinity Hall, Cambridge. Whether he treated those who came before him, lawyers or laymen, as if they were undergraduates, one cannot say. If he did, he would not differ from some other judges who have been known to act as if those who were in their Court were *in statu pupillari*. But the holding by Marriott simultaneously of an academic and of a legal post shows very well the congenial society which Johnson would find when he visited a friend in "The Commons".

Johnson has often been called a representative Englishman. A sound critic has described him as "the embodiment of the essential features of the English character". The efficient application of justice in a practical way is a national and immemorial characteristic of the English people, and the English Common Law, which is closely entwined with English habits and with the political evolution of the nation, is typical of the English mind. Johnson thoroughly appreciated it, for he had no liking for abstract theories; he was anxious that right should prevail, and at the same time he valued precedent. So, when we realize the legal qualities of Johnson's intellect, we understand better why he was representative of the British people and why he was a student and lover of the law. Indeed, we may assert that, until this side of Johnson's character has been apprehended, neither his intellect nor his life can be fully understood. It is little more than surmise, but if we examine this aspect carefully do we not discern some regret on Johnson's part that circumstances prevented him from becoming a member of the bar? It is all very well for us now, when personal values of the eighteenth century have been definitely fixed, to be sure that Johnson's fame is world-wide and permanent. But he could not see into the future, and in his lifetime Thurlow and Stowell, for example, were, even allowing for Johnson's literary reputation, men of greater eminence and of ampler fortune. Johnson knew his own capacity and could measure it with that of his contemporaries; he might well feel that fortune had been unkind to him and regret that his special qualities never had scope in the career for which they certainly fitted him.

Lord Stowell's opinion that if Johnson had become a lawyer he might have been Lord Chancellor has already been quoted. What was Johnson's reply? He became, says Boswell, agitated and angry, and exclaimed, "Why will you vex me by suggesting this when it is too late?"

# JOHNSON'S RELIGION

An incomplete view of Dr Johnson's character will be obtained if the large place which religion held in his daily life is not appreciated. His religion was part of his existence, not something extraneous to the normal progress of life, but an essential part of it, momentarily perhaps forgotten, but constantly recurring, and the subject of daily thought and meditation. Unfortunately his religion was of little comfort to Johnson. Religion was to him a divine code of conduct always in his sight, and Johnson, being but human, frequently transgressed it, and was therefore constantly repenting of his shortcomings and making good resolutions for the future.

> Lead, kindly light, amid the encircling gloom...

wrote a latter-day divine, but there was no kindly light for the Doctor spreading its gentle and soothing rays around him. He saw before him only a divine judge, as he thought, both just and merciful, and he once made this remark which reflects his own mental attitude: "There are many good men whose fear of God predominates over their love". "Have mercy upon me, my Creator and my Judge", he writes in one of his prayers. It was the reflection of his own personality, from whom he hoped for mercy; the Deity, he thought, would regard things as he did. This view of religion tended necessarily to produce mental gloom; fears and hopes sprang up together. He was always in a state of uncertainty, and so his religion was in part a distressing factor in his life.

The first of his prayers which is extant was written when Johnson was nine-and-twenty, in 1738, and the last in 1784, the year of his death, when he was seventy-five. Have any of us ever realized that for nearly half a century Johnson was in a constant state of mental distress? Or

have we noted the contrast between
Johnson as we are accustomed to see him
in the company of his friends and Johnson in the privacy of his chamber?

In a fragmentary diary covering the
latter half of March 1782, we find this
attitude of mind mingled with trivial
occurrences in a pathetic manner. On
Sunday, 17 March, Johnson writes: "I
read a Greek chapter, prayed with Francis
[Barber, the negro servant] which I now
do commonly, and explained to him The
Lord's Prayer....I made punch for
myself and my servants, by which, in the
night, I thought both my breast and
my imagination disordered." And on the
28th, the anniversary of his wife's death,
the Doctor notes, "This is the day on
which, in 1772, dear Tetty died. I have
now uttered a prayer of repentance and
contrition; perhaps Tetty knows that I
prayed for her. Perhaps Tetty is now
praying for me—God help me. Thou,
God, art merciful—hear my prayers and
enable me to trust in Thee".

The result of the thoughts of his trans-
gressions, which were ever springing up
in Johnson's mind, caused him, since he
habitually expressed his ideas either in
writing or in speech, to compose a number of prayers, nearly all of which may
be regarded as guides to his future conduct. One can read them in the little
book entitled *Prayers and Meditations,
composed by Samuel Johnson, LL.D.*,
which was first published in August 1785,[1]
by the Reverend George Strahan, Vicar
of Islington, eight months after the Doctor's death. The notebook which contained these prayers and notes, for the so-
called meditations are but fragmentary
notes, was given by Johnson to Strahan in
his last days. He probably intended the
prayers only to be published, but Strahan
printed both prayers and meditations.
Johnson consented to the publication
even of the prayers reluctantly and his re-

[1] A new edition, with an Introduction by the Rev.
H. E. Savage, D.D., Dean of Lichfield, was published
in 1927 (Lichfield, Lomax's Successors).

ligious meditations were so little intruded
on his friends—in company, he always
manfully made the best of life—that
there is something of impertinence in
discussing his thoughts on religion, his
fears and his hopes; on the other hand,
if one disregards them, one is in danger
of misapprehending his character. From
them, at any rate, we have more evidence
of Johnson's thoughts on religion than
we have of most men. They show very
plainly that Johnson was always in a
state of repentance and of resolves.
Examples are numerous, but here is one
regretting his idleness, resolving to do
better, hoping for forgiveness:

### AFTER TIME NEGLIGENTLY AND UNPROFITABLY SPENT

*November* 19, [1752].

O Lord, in whose hands are life and death,
by whose power I am sustained, and by whose
mercy I am spared, look down upon me with
pity. Forgive me, that I have this day neg-
lected the duty which Thou hast assigned to it,

and suffered the hours, of which I must give account, to pass away without any endeavour to accomplish Thy will, or to promote my own salvation. Make me to remember, O God, that every day is Thy gift, and ought to be used according to Thy command. Grant me, therefore, so to repent of my negligence, that I may obtain mercy from Thee, and pass the time which Thou shalt yet allow me in diligent performance of Thy commands, through JESUS CHRIST. Amen.

Two things are certain: first, that religion brought little comfort to Johnson. To be throughout life a religious man, as he rightly thought himself—seeking to attain perfection, yet ever hoping for pardon for his imperfection—does not tend to happiness, and Johnson was happiest not when he was thinking of religion in his own room or in the watches of the night but when he was in the society of his friends where he had forgotten all about it. Secondly, Johnson's thoughts on religion were affected by his bad health. This is frequently referred to in the prayers, but it is never so noticeable

as in the meditations or, as it is preferable
to call them, his notes. They are filled
with instances—"I was faint, dined on
herrings and potatoes", and again, "My
nights are restless and tedious and my
days drowsy. The flatulence which tor-
ments me has sometimes so obstructed
my breath that the act of respiration becomes not only voluntary but laborious
in a recumbent posture. By copious
bleeding I was relieved, but not cured".
This physical condition reacted on his
religion, causing him to regard it as a
collection of rather hard rules which he
was daily transgressing. His view was, in
fact, extraordinarily limited. He never
considered the basis of religion nor the
ethical teaching of the gospels. To him
religion was something like the British
Constitution: it was in existence and it
must regulate his conduct in life; by
it he must be eventually saved or
condemned. "If", he once said when
discussing the conversion of a young
woman to Quakerism, "you live con-

scientiously in that religion [in which you have been educated] you may be saved".

No mysticism was to be found in Johnson's religion. Religious experience possessed no varieties for him. Prayer was not an approach but was always propitiatory. With his clear and definite mental images he did not attempt to merge himself in the Infinite. Exaggerating his small human shortcomings, it seems almost pathetic that in his religion this great and good man found so little consolation, so little comfort, so little peace in spite of daily effort.

It is also very noticeable that in connection with his religion the Doctor shows a simplicity and a humility, a childlike submissiveness and an abnegation of energy, extraordinarily different from his attitude to every other subject.

No doubt many of his actions—his generosity, his kindness—were governed by the principles of his religion of which he daily reminded himself; on the other hand his robust intelligence would have realized the importance of observing sane rules of moral conduct without the perusal of the scriptures in his home. Be this as it may, religion, Johnson's narrow religion, was an element in his life, the importance of which it is impossible to exaggerate.

The irony of the situation is that he was a good man who regulated all his actions by religious precepts, a man who did not leave his religion behind him in the church of St Clement Danes, a man whose sins, if such they can be called, were trivial—late rising and want of diligence—a man who was yet constantly anxious as to his religious state. When therefore we see the Doctor at the Literary Club or at Streatham, engaged in controversy and friendly argument, laying down the law and recalling literary incidents which he drew from his capacious memory, we must always remember that there was a sombre background to the attractive scene and that there was another side to his character, that of the sincerely religious man doubtful or disturbed beyond measure by a self-exaggeration of his shortcomings and of the uncertainty of the future.

# § II

## SOME COMPARISONS

*Johnson and Windham*
*Johnson and Selden*
*Johnson and Anatole France*
*Johnson and Wordsworth in the Highlands*

# JOHNSON AND WINDHAM

On 5 April 1784 William Windham—
"Mr Windham of Norfolk"—was elected
member for the City of Norwich, and
from his ability, character, and ample
fortune, became a prominent adherent of
the Whig Party. In 1794, however, when
the Duke of Portland and the majority
of the Whig leaders formed a coalition
with Pitt, he became Secretary of State
for War and a member of the Cabinet;
subsequently, until his death, he was a
conspicuous public and parliamentary
figure.

In Windham's early and non-political
life his friendship with Dr Johnson is an
outstanding and impressive feature, the
only feature, in fact, to distinguish it
from the lives of other young men of
fortune and family at the end of the
eighteenth century. As the years pass by

and the value of many political events becomes historically minimized, this friendship emerges as a permanent and important literary episode, its value increasing rather than diminishing with time. It is an example of Johnson's mental liberality and open-mindedness, for without these traits a friendship between an old and a young man is impossible. When Johnson died in December 1784, he was seventy-five and Windham was thirty-four; there was, therefore, forty years' difference, as near as may be, between them. The common ground on which this unusual union was based may perhaps be found in the profound appreciation which each of them had of the value of morality and intellect.

Of Johnson's religious faith many instances might be given, familiar to every reader of Boswell's *Life*. Windham, too, was a religious man, anxious for his spiritual welfare, an instance of which is to be found in his diary for 1 September

1784, where is this entry: "Left Ashbourne at half-past one, having gone with Dr Johnson in the morning to prayers".

Windham's diary[1] is full also of examples of an enthusiasm for, and devotion to, literature and science, and he regarded intellectual society as a necessary element in a well-ordered life. On 25 March 1785, after breakfasting with Sir Joshua Reynolds, he wrote in his diary: "Reflected while I was there on the strange state of my past life, in which time was either wanting, or supposed to be wanting, for such company as I was then in". In an earlier entry (10 January) he refers to a dinner of which he remarks that he remained "partaking more of the pleasures of the company and conversation than I can often remember to have done till now". When we realize Windham's introspective character, his moral ideas, his searchings of heart combined

---

[1] The published part of the diary begins in 1784; the portions before that date, except from 1772 to 1775, seem to have been lost.

with love of learning, of conversation and of society, we can see how Johnson must have attracted him. How permanent was the value which Windham set on Johnson's opinions is exemplified by a characteristic entry in his diary of 6 April 1785, when, after noting that the evening was spent chiefly in thinking on work, he continues that the latter part of it was passed "in doing what I have so often thought of and never performed, and of which the trial shows that the neglect is to be severely regretted—namely, in getting by heart part of Johnson's writings. The present instance was No. 104 of the *Rambler*".

While some kindred interests were essential as grounds of this friendship, it could not have developed into one so deep and affectionate but for Johnson's kindliness on one side and Windham's warm respect on the other. He regarded Johnson as his master in morals, as he looked on Burke as his master in politics. In the last interview but one between them, on 7 December 1784, Windham, after Johnson had characteristically urged him to set apart every seventh day for the care of his soul, and had confided his servant Frank to his care, rather pedantically desired to obtain his opinion on natural and revealed religion, which he says was "in part gratified on the instant". The interest of this episode is in the fact that it illustrates the pupil desiring instruction from the master, and the master giving it—on his death-bed.

The last interview between these friends, on 12 December, has, like that of 7 December, been fully described by the detailed entries to be found in Windham's diary. Master and pupil have by this time disappeared and we see only two friends. "I then said that I hoped he would forgive my earnestness or something to that effect, when he replied eagerly, 'that from me nothing would be necessary by way of apology', adding with great fervour in words which I shall (I hope) never forget, 'God

R                                    4

bless you my dear Windham through Jesus Christ' ''.

The death of Dr Johnson in December 1784 was the end of this friendship. When and how did it begin?

As a friendship it did not begin before 1778, when on 11 December, proposed by Sheridan and seconded by Bennet Langton, Windham was elected a member of the famous Literary Club, and on 18 December was present at the first dinner after his election. From this time he was well known to Johnson.

On this point it is as well to refer to a few dates before 1778. Windham went down from Oxford in 1771, and in 1773 he started on an adventure, for he left England on a voyage with Commodore Phipps to discover a northern route to India. This expedition was a fiasco so far as Windham was concerned, for, suffering very much from sea-sickness, he left the ship in the North Sea and was landed at Bergen; it was not till the end of the year that he was again in England. From that

time until the beginning of 1778 Windham seems to have lived between Norfolk and London. There are, in fact,
entries in his diaries which show that in
February 1774 and January 1775 he was
in London, and in January 1778 he took
part in public meetings against the war
with the American Colonies, a step in
which we may trace the influence of
Burke. But from the end of 1778 and
beginning of 1779 to September 1780,
Windham was abroad in Switzerland and
Italy for his health. If this time be elimi-
nated, his friendship with Johnson ex-
tended over quite a short period—only
from 1780 to 1784.

In the *Windham Papers* published in
1913 it is stated by the anonymous editor
(p. 62) that "it is clear from Boswell's
*Life* that as early as 1776 they were on
intimate terms". This statement is not
accurate. The first mention of Windham
in Boswell's *Life* is in 1775, when this
sentence occurs, "he expressed to his
friend Mr Windham of Norfolk his won-

der at the extreme jealousy of the Scotch". This particular portion of Boswell's *Life* refers to the recently published *Journey* to the Hebrides, but it does not follow that Johnson's remark to Windham was made at this time, namely 1775. It may have been, and probably was, spoken years later, and it is only brought in at this place by Boswell because he was then writing about the Hebrides and Scotland.

But by the middle of 1774, though not yet a friend in the full sense, Windham had some kind of acquaintance with Johnson. Extracts from Windham's early diaries—from 1772 to 1775—are printed by the Historical Manuscripts Commission among the Ketton MSS., and under date of July 1774, though the exact day is not given, there is this entry:

On road from Derby to Matlock:
We met Mr Thrale's coach in which was Johnson, who assented to the remark of the extreme beauty of the country, and observed that it was an object of reasonable curiosity, the situation of the house here and the whole scene just like Bristol, July 1–16, 1774.

From this entry one may infer that this was not the first meeting between Johnson and Windham. Windham's entries are always scrappy and of a pocket-book character, and Johnson's remarks at the meeting must have been jotted down somewhat inaccurately, from memory, for why should Johnson say that "a beautiful scene" is an object of "reasonable curiosity"? However, in this entry we have evidence that Johnson and Windham were acquainted in 1774. On the other hand, that acquaintance cannot yet have been worthy of the name of friendship. It is equally clear, however, that Windham already appreciated and valued Johnson's words, for it was not his habit to note conversation in his diary.

This meeting occurred during Johnson's tour to Wales in 1774 with the Thrales, and they were in Derbyshire from 9 to 20 July. During that tour both Johnson and Mrs Thrale kept a diary, and in each several names occur, but there is no mention in either of the meeting with Windham. This, again, is evidence that Johnson's acquaintance with Windham at this time was very slight, and that Windham was not regarded either by Johnson or Mrs Thrale as a person who interested them; he was only young Mr Windham of Norfolk, otherwise they would hardly have failed to mention so pleasant an encounter in the wilds of Derbyshire. It is also significant that in 1778, when Windham was elected to the Literary Club, Johnson neither proposed nor seconded him, though the Doctor was at the dinner on 27 November, when the names were put up for election at the following dinner, and took part in the proposal of two other candidates.[1] Therefore we come back to December 1778 as the time when the friendship between the Doctor and Windham began.

Johnson was by universal consent one

[1] The information as to the proceedings of the Club has been kindly supplied by Sir Frederick Kenyon, K.C.B., the present Treasurer of the Club.

of the best talkers of his time, and Windham had also a unique reputation among
his contemporaries—men and women—
for his conversation. The cause of its
charm it is now impossible to know, for
written records cannot disclose the
nuances of a friendly dialogue; but it
probably arose from intellectual versa-
tility combined with a sympathetic manner. To the first Wraxall seems plainly to
refer when he writes of Windham that
"his conversation displayed the treasures
of a highly cultivated intellect". Windham was obviously gifted with an inherent capacity of adaptation; with Johnson he could be pleasantly serious, with
Fanny Burney vivacious without famili-
arity, with Mrs Crewe easy and sensible.
One may assume also that he let his
friends talk about themselves and was
never egotistical himself; he kept his
own troubles and pleasures for the pages
of his diary.

One remembers how Johnson appreciated Thurlow because, as he said,

he "put his mind to yours". Windham had, no doubt, the gift of stimulating expression in others, and as this was combined with appropriate replies his conversation appeared admirable, and was thoroughly appreciated by Johnson. In a letter to Dr Brocklesby, written from Ashbourne on 2 September 1784, Johnson said, "Mr Windham has been here to see me, he came, I think, forty miles out of his way, and stayed about a day and a half. Such conversation I shall not have again till I come back to the regions of literature, and there Windham is *inter stellas luna minores*".

A point in regard to this quotation is not without interest, though it is not strictly relevant to this narrative. Birkbeck Hill says that it is surprising that so excellent a scholar as Dr Johnson did not quote the lines of Horace correctly. In the original the word "ignes" is found, and not "stellas". But may not Johnson have used the word "stellas" intentionally? Was he adapting the poet's words to his own purpose and not quoting him textually? Was he not thinking of the talkers whom he met at the Club—of Garrick, Burke, Reynolds, Stowell and others, who were all conversational stars? Among these bright but lesser constellations Windham was as a moon. If we look at the words from this point of view, how much more vivid is "stellas" than "ignes", though for the purpose of scansion it is incorrect. But Johnson was not passing an examination, he was writing a letter, and the Latin words, as he wrote them, aptly expressed his meaning, more aptly than if he had used the indefinite word "ignes".

When Fanny Burney was present on 13 February 1788, at the opening of the trial of Warren Hastings, Windham was introduced to her. She was so opposed to the trial that she disliked the idea of this introduction, but she overcame it when she remembered the friendship which had existed between Windham and her old friend. It was for us a fortunate meeting, as it caused Fanny to write a graphic sketch of the relations between Windham and Johnson.

He loved Dr Johnson—and Dr Johnson returned his affection. Their political principles and connections were opposite, but Mr Windham respected his venerable friend too highly to discuss any points that could offend him; and showed for him so true a regard that, during all his late illnesses for the latter part of his life, his carriage and himself were alike at his service, to air, visit, or go out, whenever he was disposed to accept them. Nor was this all; one tender proof he gave of warm and generous regard, that I can never forget, and that rose instantly to my mind when I heard his name and gave him a welcome in my eyes when they met his face: it is this: Dr Johnson in his last visit to Lichfield, was taken ill and waited to recover strength for travelling back to town in his usual vehicle, a stage coach: as soon as this reached the ears of Mr Windham, he set off for Lichfield in his own carriage, to offer to bring him back to town in it and at his own time.

For a young man of fashion such a trait, towards an old, however dignified, philosopher, must surely be a mark indisputable of an elevated mind and character; and still the more strongly

it marked a noble way of thinking, as it was done
in favour of a person in open opposition to
all his own party and declared prejudices.[1]

In this sketch two sentences are noteworthy. One reveals a detail of Johnson's life at the end of his days. "His
carriage and himself were alike at his service, to air, visit, or go out, whenever he
was disposed to accept them".

In his diary on 15 May 1784 Windham
notes: "Dined at three with Dr Brocklesby; present, Dr Johnson, Vallancey,
William Smith (Member for Sudbury),
Deveynes (the apothecary), Boswell,
Murphy and somebody else". He then
continues: "After dinner took Johnson
an airing over Blackfriars Bridge, then
to the Club: present, Boswell, Murphy,
Brocklesby, Barry, Mr Bowles, Hook
and his son, and a son of Dr Burney, he
that was expelled Cambridge".

Johnson being driven about London
in Windham's fashionable carriage is not
a picture which we have hitherto visual-

[1] *Diary of Madame d'Arblay* (13 Feb. 1788).

ized, nor has the affectionate and unremitting attention of Windham to Johnson in this last year of the Doctor's life been quite appreciated. The value which Johnson attached to it we know from a passage in his undated letter to Windham, of August, in which he speaks of the tenderness with which Windham had treated him through his long illness which "neither health nor sickness can ever make me forget". Unremitting seems a suitable description when we recall some entries in Windham's diary for 1784. On 19 January he "went immediately to see Dr Johnson", and "sat about an hour and a half with him". On the 21st "About eight I set out for Dr Johnson's, who not being well enough to admit me, I called at the Pay Office". On the 25th Windham again called but was not admitted, and on 7 February comes the regretful entry, "Have not seen Dr Johnson since 19th ultimo, i.e. to the present day, inclusive nineteen days".

With all Windham's desire for the

society of Johnson he could not have seen much of him in 1784 after the entry of 15 May, for the Doctor left London for Ashbourne on 13 July and did not return to London until 16 November. During this time Windham and Johnson only met when Windham visited him at Ashbourne in the autumn, and, in the brief space of life which remained to Johnson after his return, his health was so bad that Windham saw little of his friend in spite of his wish to be with him. But it was Windham's servant who attended him in his last days.

The other noteworthy remark in Miss Burney's diary is: "Mr Windham respected his venerable friend too highly to discuss any points that could offend him". Boswell has enabled us to observe how Windham avoided irritating his "venerable friend". How he drove over Blackfriars Bridge and then to dinner at the Essex Head Club has just been told. In the *Life* we have a description of the evening of this same day—5 May—when after the pleasant airing Johnson was "in fine spirits". In the course of the evening he made some disparaging remarks about Burke's conversation when the statesman tried to be merry, with which Windham told Boswell that he did not agree. But did he begin to argue with the sage? Not at all. "It would not", said Boswell, "have been right for either of us to have contradicted Johnson at this time...it might have occasioned something more rough, and at any rate would have checked the flow of Johnson's good humour".

Obviously Windham stimulated Johnson without irritating him, and thus obtained all the benefit of his vast knowledge and power of expression, much to his own edification, whilst Johnson in his turn regarded Windham, who avoided points which could annoy his venerable friend, as pre-eminent among conversationalists.

But what a tribute the attitude of Windham to Johnson is to the value of tact. Tact is a product of sensitiveness, and Windham, as we can perceive from his diary and from other evidence, was a very sensitive man, and to this element in his nature we may in some degree attribute the friendship between Johnson and himself, for it enabled him to admire without adulation, and to argue without annoying.

When the diarist contrasts the philosopher and the young man of fashion, she forgets that Johnson was essentially a man of the world, and that Windham's liking for field sports, horse-racing, and boxing, would amuse and even please Johnson. "I am sorry", the Doctor once remarked, "that prize-fighting is gone out, every art should be preserved, and the art of defence is surely important". He would have been consoled if he could have read Windham's description of the fight between a butcher and a Jew at Bristol in 1788, and of other pugilistic combats which the statesman watched with the eye of a connoisseur.

When Madame d'Arblay praises Windham for his kindness to Johnson, as he
was a man differing from him in political
opinion, she seems to forget the friendship of other Whigs, notably Fox and
Burke, for Johnson. But, be that as it
may, this friendship of Windham for the
Doctor is unforgettable, for it is an
outstanding event in the last year of
Johnson's life, and will also, as the years
go by, remain a lasting memorial of a
statesman whose public actions are now
almost forgotten.

# JOHNSON AND SELDEN

ONE need not seek for a precise defini-
tion of the words "table talk"; true
"table talk" is informal, spoken among
friends at a dinner table or by the fire-
side. It must be natural and spontaneous,
revealing in a flash the mind of the speaker
at the moment. If it becomes narrative,
drifting into anecdotes or homilies, it
ceases to be table talk, which must be
brief and pointed, and, while there should
be a savour of sagacity and shrewdness,
it should contain learning without dull-
ness or pedantry and knowledge of the
world without degenerating into gossip.
Some so-called table talk, which has
been preserved, differs from such as is
comprised in this description. That of
Coleridge consisted of extracts from
monologues often spoken from his bed,
"an exhaustive, cyclical mode of dis-
coursing, unfit indeed for a dinner table

R                                                5

and too long breathed for the patience of a chance visitor". The collection of the table talk of Samuel Rogers, which was compiled by J. M. Dyce, is a collection almost entirely of anecdotes and reminiscences and there are none of the mordant thrusts which Rogers' friends disliked as much as they admired his generosity; these would certainly have amused men of a later generation.

Obviously "table talk", however entertaining, can seldom be preserved and must be lost unless someone with a retentive memory will take the trouble not only to remember, but also to record it as it was spoken. It is fortunate for those who have lived after them that Selden's in the seventeenth, and Johnson's in the eighteenth century have been methodically preserved in unique and substantial measure.

Strangely enough Boswell, a Scotch lawyer, has done this for a great English man of letters, Samuel Johnson, and

Richard Milward, a divine who died a canon of Windsor and was for many years his secretary, has performed the same task for John Selden, the famous jurist, scholar and statesman who, though he had a divine for secretary, was certainly not a friend of the clergy. Both narrators went about their task systematically and there has now been published a facsimile of one of the many notebooks in which Boswell jotted down at night his recollection of Johnson's talk during the previous hours.[1] Milward was evidently also a careful chronicler, though we have no record such as that of Boswell which is now in America in the library of Mr R. B. Adam; we merely have his own statement in his short prefatory letter to Selden's executors which was attached to the first edition of the *Table Talk* of 1689, that he "faithfully committed to writing" and "digested in-

[1] *Boswell's Note Book*, 1776–1777 . . . *now first published from the unique original in the collection of R. B. Adam*, London, 1925.

to this method" various sayings of Selden, and that he tabulated under distinct headings the "excellent" words which fell from his patron.

Between the two narrators and their work there is this difference, that while much is known about Boswell's life from his books and correspondence, of Milward as a man we are entirely ignorant.

We know that Milward collected the table talk of Selden during the last twenty years of that eminent man's life. He heard, he says, his discourse twenty years together. Selden died in 1654, so that the period of the record would be from 1634 onwards. All we learn of Milward is that at this time he was rector of Braxted in Essex but, as he continued to hold this preferment after he was appointed to a canonry at Windsor in 1666 and to the living of Isleworth in 1678, he would not seem to have given much, if any, personal attention to his clerical duties in Essex. So he may very well have been able to act more or less continuously as Selden's secretary, whether Selden was living at Wrest, the Earl of Kent's house in Bedfordshire, or, after the earl's death in 1639, at the house in London of Lady Kent, to whom, according to rumour, he was privately married. It was most likely at this mansion in Whitefriars, *museum meum Carmeliticum*, where Selden stored his valuable and numerous antiquities, that Milward heard most of the talk which he recorded; for fifteen years elapsed between the death of the Earl of Kent and that of Selden, and during this time the house in Whitefriars was his home.

When we come to consider the talkers, we note that Johnson and Selden, though one was solely a man of letters and the other was not only a learned scholar but also a statesman and man of action, had several similar characteristics, intellectual and moral. Each had an abnormal capacity of absorbing and of assimilating knowledge. "He was of so

stupendous learning", says Lord Claren-
don of Selden, "in all kinds and in all
languages that a man would have thought
he had been entirely conversant among
books, and had never spent an hour but
in reading and writing". The same acute
observer adds: "In his conversation he
was the most clear discourser and had the
best faculty in making hard things easy,
and presenting them to the understanding of any man that hath been known".
Every friend of Johnson admired the
same qualities in him, his store of learning and the clearness and precision of his
statements.

When we are noting resemblances in
the characters of these two eminent men
we may observe at times a distinct strain
of gaiety in each. The literary work of
both was of a serious kind. A *History of
Tithes* and the celebrated *Mare Clausum*,
in which was claimed jurisdiction for
England over all the ocean near coasts,
of the one, the *Dictionary* of the other
were not books to raise a smile. In

the Doctor bad health and melancholy
introspection obscured a gaiety which
certainly existed in his nature. But
sometimes with the right sort of friends
it was evident—with Mrs Thrale, with
Goldsmith and with Fanny Burney who
says: "He has more fun and comical
humour and love of nonsense about him
than almost any one I ever saw". We
know nothing of the intimate friends of
Selden, so we can only perceive this
brighter side of his character from
glimpses of it in his table talk.

Milward naturally tried to preserve
Selden's weighty sayings on important
subjects which did not lend themselves
to light treatment, but still from time to
time we see gleams of gaiety which no
doubt played over subjects of less importance in moments of relaxation.
"Humility", said Selden one day, "is
a virtue all men preach, none practise and
yet everybody is content to hear; the
master thinks it good doctrine for his
servant, the laity for the clergy and the

clergy for the laity". And another time he remarked,

We measure the Excellencie of other men by some Excellencie we conceive to be in ourselfes. Nash, a poett, poor enough, seeing an Alderman with his gold Chain upon his great horse, by way of scorne said to one of his Companions "Doe you see yon ffellow, how goodly, how big he looks, why, that fellow cannott make a Blank verse".

But in these lighter moods Johnson was more kindly than Selden, more the man of feeling, though not less observant of the weaknesses of his fellow-men than his predecessor. Selden, though he held quite definite opinions, was a more detached observer than Johnson, equally conscious, but less tolerant, of the follies of the world, a smiling but somewhat cynical critic.

Whitelock in his *Memorials* notes another feature in the character of Selden in which he resembles Dr Johnson, when he says of him that "he was as hospitable and generous as any man and as good company to those whom he liked". Here

we are reminded of many well-remem-
bered instances of Johnson's friendly
spirit to those whom he liked and his
many acts of kindness. In fact there
could not be a better description of some
traits in Johnson than the line and a half
in which Ben Jonson referred to Selden,
how he

> watched men, manners too,
> Heard what times past have said, seen what
> ours do.

When Johnson reported, in his own
fashion, parliamentary debates, wrote
prefaces and pamphlets and talked with
Fox and Burke he was essentially as much
an observer of the contemporary scene as
Selden, and when Whitelock speaks of
Selden's clear discourse and of his faculty
for representing facts so as to be easily
understood, one calls to mind innumer-
able instances of the same characteristics
in the Doctor.

But Selden had an advantage in the
matter of hospitality over Johnson.
Though the latter enjoyed a good dinner

and the society of his friends, he could not, like Selden, dispense hospitality in his own house, except a cup of tea, and the "society of learned men" had usually to be sought around the dinner table of his friends or at one of his clubs. One would like to read details of the symposia which Selden enjoyed; but, thanks to Boswell, we know much of Johnson's. What a day of talk, for instance, was 7 or 19 May 1773, for there is uncertainty about the date. It began with a breakfast and some talk at Henry Thrale's in the Borough; then followed a dinner at the Dillys', the booksellers in the Poultry, where there was a party of eleven; the talk was long, animated and varied. Finally the Doctor, Boswell and Langton adjourned to the Club where they found Burke, Garrick and others of the Johnson circle, and the discussions were continued. In May 1782, to come to a later period, Johnson and Boswell again dined at the Dillys' and there met Wilkes; he and Johnson, two men opposite in all respects, finished the entertainment by sitting close together in intimate conversation. To take one more example, Boswell tells how on the memorable expedition to the Hebrides he and his companion arrived at Tobermory in the island of Mull, when "Dr Johnson and I sat by ourselves at the inn and talked a good deal".

Every one of these occasions, not to mention many others, gave opportunities for Johnsonian table talk and we can picture the Doctor without difficulty, among the books at the Dillys' or before a peat fire in Mull and almost hear his forcible conversation.

Mr Paul, in his entertaining sketch of Selden,[1] has gone so far as to assert that Johnson based his style of talk on that of Selden. That he had an uncommon appreciation of his predecessor we know, but the strong homely sense which is so evident in the table talk of each of these famous men was the product of their par-

[1] *Men and Letters*, 1901.

ticular intellectual character, clearness of vision, dislike of obscurity of statement and some contempt for those with less vigorous understandings. To think of Johnson endeavouring, when a vivid thought flashed through his mind, to consider how he should make a statement after the manner of Selden, is really to fail in appreciation of Johnson's intellect and temper.

For modern readers Johnson has two distinct advantages over Selden: his world, moral, political and social, is nearer to our own, and therefore his talk falls on more receptive ground and is preserved in a very human atmosphere. For, in nearly every instance, we know something of the surroundings and of the company in which the sayings were spoken. But we have to imagine Selden with his sharp oval face, long nose, full grey eyes and flowing hair, stiffly dressed and seated among the formal furniture of the seventeenth century—altogether in an atmosphere much more ceremonious than that of the Turk's Head or of Streatham.

Though the form in which Milward preserved the sayings which he thought should be remembered is precise and severe, as compared with Boswell's atmosphere of genial individuality, the general basis of the talk of Selden and Johnson was similar. Each penetrated rapidly to the heart of a subject and at once expressed the result with a clearness and incisiveness which made it plain to the ordinary man. It is true that each had his strong prejudices. Johnson, for instance, hated Whigs and Whiggery and took every opportunity to say so. When Boswell spoke of Grainger's *Biographical Dictionary*, "The Dog is a Whig, I do not like much to see a Whig in any dress", observed Johnson. Selden also had his dislikes. He never, for example, hid his contempt for the clergy generally, and for bishops in particular. "Chain up the Clergy on both sides", is his contemptuous remark in reference to the failure of negotiations between Charles I and Parliament; and here we may see evidence of the acute controversies of the time. Of bishops who were preachers, he remarks in a homely fashion just as Dr Johnson might have done, "for a bishop to preach 'tis to do other folks' office, as if the steward of the house should execute the porter's or the cook's place, 'tis his business to see that they and all others about the house perform their duties".

When, however, we discard or make allowances for prejudices (and from these no one is altogether free), we find in the table talk of the man of letters and of the legal antiquary a store-house of home truths which live because they permanently apply to human action to-day as much as in the seventeenth and eighteenth centuries.

"Of all actions of a man's life", said Selden, "his marriage does least concern other people, yet of all actions of our life 'tis most meddled with by other people".

This true and witty observation can be matched by one of Johnson's which is probably equally true.

"When I censured a gentleman of my acquaintance", says Boswell, "for marrying a second time, as it shewed a disregard of his first wife, he said, 'Not at all, sir. On the contrary, were he not to marry again, it might be concluded that his first wife had given him a disgust to marriage; but by taking a second wife he pays the highest compliment to the first by shewing that she made him so happy as a married man that he wishes to be so a second time'".

On another occasion during tea in his house in Johnson Court, when there was much talk, Johnson remarked, somewhat too sweepingly but yet with considerable truth, "It is not from reason and prudence that people marry but from inclination". Sometimes one finds that the two men differed on the same point. Selden has a good deal to say about preachers, "Preaching by the Spirit (as they call it) is most esteemed by the common people, because they cannot abide art or learning". With this statement most men will agree but Johnson did not, and so when he was told that he had talked above the capacity of some people his reply was, "No matter, sir, they consider it a compliment to be talked to as if they were wiser than they are. So true is this, sir, that Baxter made it a rule in every sermon that he preached to say something that was above the capacity of his audience". Selden's table talk on the subject of preachers and preaching abounds in pointed and sometimes rather ironical sayings. He was, like many eminent men of the seventeenth century, deeply interested in the ecclesiastical and moral controversies of the time, while to Johnson the subject was but of passing interest.

Milward naturally made a selection of those of Selden's sayings which seemed to him most worth preserving and, from his own position as a divine, he would be inclined to choose those which touched on the political and ecclesiastical affairs of the day. Indeed, he says of Selden in

his letter to the executors, "With a mar-
vellous delight to those that heard him,
he would presently convey the highest
points of religion and the most important affairs of state to an ordinary ap-
prehension". The table talk of Selden
which has been preserved is therefore not
so varied as that of Johnson, but equally
with that of the Doctor it is an aid to the
appreciation of the speaker's personality.
Thus, thanks to Boswell and Milward
and their records, we understand Johnson and Selden better than we do most
men who have attained to eminence in
the past. Their table talk has an even
wider interest for us, for, in the unpremeditated words of Selden and Johnson,
we perceive in plain and familiar terms a
reflection of the opinion and thought of
the ages in which they lived.

# JOHNSON AND ANATOLE FRANCE

At first sight it appears startling to couple Dr Johnson and Anatole France, men of letters of different nationality who lived in separate centuries. Yet it is neither difficult nor uninteresting to find some remarkable similarities between these two famous figures, not as men of letters, but as personalities, each of whom had, towards the end of his days, obtained a unique place in the intellectual and social life of his age. One was the "Great Cham of Literature", the other was "Le Maître"—the Master. Each name is significant of a dominant place held not only among intellectual persons but among ordinarily intelligent men.

Mrs Thrale has a story that one day, as the Doctor was walking along the Strand, a gentleman stepped out of a neighbouring tavern, his napkin in his hand and without a hat and, stopping him as civilly as he could, said, "I beg your pardon, sir; but you are Dr Johnson, I believe". "Yes, sir". "We have a wager depending on your reply: pray, sir, is it 'irrèparable' or 'irrepàirable' that one should say"? The Doctor gave his decision and passed on. Whether the story be true or not makes little difference, for it would not have been current and preserved by Mrs Thrale, but for the extraordinary position which Johnson had secured. Johnson and France had attained this special place in a large measure by a form of literary work, common to each, in which the dissemination of ideas was capable of absorption by ordinary folk.

Dr Johnson enunciated his opinions in the *Rambler* and the *Idler* and in *Rasselas*, but the publication of the *Dictionary* in 1747 had given him a peculiar public reputation which caused his subsequent essays to become at once

more authoritative and more popular.
France moralized in a more subtle form
—in novels and through the conversation and opinions of Monsieur Bergeret
and the Abbé Coignard; these characters
were to all intents and purposes Anatole
France and were accepted by the public
as such. But it was the capacity for ex-
position in society which finally gave
both Johnson and France their special
position. They are alike in the supreme
confidence with which they dictated to
the world, without which they would not
have become oracles at the end of their
lives. While each was equally sure of his
opinions, each was equally often wrong.
Dr Johnson on the war with the American Colonists was frequently as wrong-
headed as Anatole France often was,
when he discussed the origin and progress of the Great War. The intervention
of the United States, for example, France
regarded as caused by political and
financial self-interest. The American
generals who visited him at Tours he

considered as being rather more stupid
than those in command of the French
forces. "Joffre", he said cynically one
day, "learnt of the victory of the Marne
from the *Petit Parisien*".

It is in their individual influence in
society that the chief resemblance between Johnson and France can be found,
for with the exception of the *Lives of the
Poets*, the *Journey to the Western Isles*
and a few small pieces, Johnson's work
was completed with the publication of
*Rasselas* when he was but fifty years of
age. France, on the contrary, continued
to work almost to the time of his death
in 1924. But from 1759 to the end of his
life Johnson was obtaining a new and
more autocratic place through the exercise
of conversational gifts when presiding
among his fellows. France talked in the
*salon* of the Villa Said at Versailles, and,
from 1914 to the beginning of his last
illness, in the *salon* of La Béchellerie, the
house close to Tours in the village of St
Cyr-sur-Loire, which he purchased on

the outbreak of the war. Often he was to
be found in the back room of the *librairie
Tridon* in Tours. Here, seated on a
high couch, with his walking-stick between his legs and gesticulating with his
tortoise-shell glasses, he would spend
hours in conversation, his attentive and
admiring audience seated around him on a
long counter covered with green leather.
For years, on Sunday afternoons at Versailles or Tours, he was the centre of a
circle of friends and casual visitors, the
latter of all nationalities, many of them
strangers who remained only a few
moments, saw the Master and obtained
from him his autograph in one of his
books, and then disappeared. Without
the love of society and of conversation
which were predominant traits both in
Johnson and France, no amount of purely
literary fame would have given them their
national reputations.

In conversation Johnson and France
were alike in their outspoken opinions
of individual men—a fact which added

not a little to the enjoyment of their visitors; probably the personal views of no literary men of eminence have been so largely preserved and circulated. They lent themselves to immortality and to permanence, for they were always clear, decided, and epigrammatic. "Sir", Dr Johnson once said of Goldsmith, "he is so much afraid of being unnoticed that he often talks merely lest you should forget he is in the company". And he said of Burke that he was not so agreeable as the variety of his knowledge would otherwise make him, because he talked partly from ostentation. This may be compared with France's cynical remark on Louis Barthou: "He has delivered an admirable oration on Napoleon, but he could quite well have spoken to the contrary, for he is a man who changes opportunely". "Heredia", he observed of the poet, "collected words as children collect pebbles; he picks out words from dictionaries", and more to the same effect, and then, with Johnsonian good nature and frankness, he concluded "After all, he is the best fellow in the world".

Most of France's sayings were tinged with cynicism or with good-natured irony. "A people must be very rich to indulge in the luxury of a democratic government"; and of a friend who was an anarchist he said that he liked him because, never having taken part in the government of his country, he was still very innocent. Another time he caustically observed that "Intelligence is a calamity; it is the worst gift anyone can have in the world". The French word "intelligence" is too limited for English readers, but one may perhaps call it "brains", and a good many will agree with France's corollary that "the true dream is to be stupid, which, however, does not exclude skill"—in other words, the manual worker, undisturbed by mental storms, doubts, and searchings, is happier than many of the modern brain-workers.

In the range and retentiveness of their

memory, we find a marked resemblance between the two men. Johnson preserved in his mind all sorts of out-of-the-way verses, which in the first instance he could hardly have done more than scan in a hasty reading. Similarly, France could recite without effort hundreds of lines of Racine and André Chénier, and he knew by heart endless details gathered from histories and memoirs, to which he could refer in conversation without effort and with surprising accuracy. Johnson and France are not the only persons who have had this same fortunate natural endowment. But in their case, as in that of Macaulay, the gift was employed in public; it was not reserved only for the society of a friend, or the creation of a book. Johnson was very contemptuous of a scholar who was silent in society. Referring to Demosthenes Taylor, he exclaimed in his vehement way, "He will not talk, sir, so his learning does no good—gives us no pleasure". France, whose disciples were more numerous than those of Johnson, was ever willing to give them both the benefit and the pleasure of his accumulated store of learning. This utilization of an extraordinary memory in conversation unites the Doctor and the Master. Each spoke to a circle, one at Streatham, at a club or in some hospitable house, the other at the Villa Said at Versailles, or at La Béchellerie, and each with equal enjoyment. "There is in the world", the Doctor once declared, "no real delight but exchange of ideas in conversation", a sentiment with which France would have agreed, though both of these great men reduced, or were sometimes allowed by their friends to reduce, conversation to a monologue, so that often there was little of that exchange of ideas which Johnson regarded as the basis of true conversation. Bennet Langton, after an evening with Johnson and Burke, was walking home with the statesman, and in the course of their talk Langton said that he could have wished, during the evening, to have heard more from another person, meaning Burke. "Oh no", said Burke, "it is enough for me to have rung the bell". Johnson had, on that occasion, obviously monopolized the conversation.

The same conversational fault is equally discernible in the familiar descriptions which have been written since his death of the intimate life of France. Those who listened to him, says Maurice Le Goff, dared not express an opinion contrary to what he had stated. Both men became in fact autocrats in conversation, not from arrogance or egotism but because their special gifts—rapid assimilation of knowledge, keen observation, vivid interest in all around them, and a remarkable facility and accuracy of expression, gave them a dominating influence in a social circle. It would have been impossible for a man of great intellectual gifts, delighting in their display among men and women, not to have fallen into this weakness, especially when it is clear that France made no attempt to limit the

number of his guests. So far from re-
tiring from the crowd, he welcomed it;
and yet, curiously enough, he disliked
and evaded public meetings.

This pleasure in society, of course, laid
both men open to the advances of those
stupid people whom both Johnson and
France rather liked to snub. A lady, for
instance, asked France one day which of
his books he preferred, and he replied
without a moment's hesitation, *Le Violon
de Faïence*—a delightful story, not however by Anatole France, but by Champ-
fleury, an admirable writer, published in
1862. The reply came with equal rapidity,
"Moi aussi, Maître". Boswell has noted
quite similar sallies by Johnson, though
his replies to foolish people were more in
the nature of blows with a bludgeon.
"Would you", asked a young gentleman
in the drawing-room at Streatham, "advise me to marry"? The answer startled
the ingenuous inquirer. "I would advise
no man to marry, sir, who is not likely to
propagate understanding", and he walked

out of the room. "Our companion", observes Mrs Thrale, "looked confounded".

It would be a mistake, however, to regard the pleasure which Johnson and France found in society merely as an idle way of passing an hour or two, or of exhibiting remarkable mental gifts. It was largely a form of philanthropy— that is, not of philanthropy as popularly regarded, limited to the assistance of some benevolent object, but in a finer sense; a love of their fellow-beings, of coming in contact with them, of finding enjoyment in their gifts and even in their faults. It was the result of large-heartedness. Johnson was a strong Tory, but he had intimate friends among the Whigs. France, who could see all the shortcomings of democracy, was actually in theory a socialist, chiefly from the same reason—a desire to see everyone as well off as himself.

In another and an admirable way there was a distinct affinity between Johnson and France. Each detested exaggeration in statement and big words, whether in conversation or in writing.

A phrase which France used, and which includes a neat play on words, illustrative of this statement has been preserved by one of France's most assiduous listeners during the last decade of his life. "Les grands mots, mon ami, mènent aux grands maux." It is not surprising that one who was always seeking in writing for the *mot juste*, and who valued form in literature, should have disliked exaggeration of verbal expression as much as Johnson, and it was for this reason that in conversation France spoke carefully, and even with some hesitation.

As for Johnson, Boswell has given many examples of this dislike. In fact, he has told a story on the point against himself, for at Harwich when Boswell was starting on his journey to Utrecht and observed that it would be terrible if the Doctor could not, after he had sailed, speedily return to London, the latter reproved him with the remark, "Don't, sir, accustom yourself to use big words for little matters"; and he gave for a reason for liking old Mr Langton that "he never embraces you with an over-acted cordiality"—a cordiality, that is, of language.

The resemblances between Johnson and Anatole France clearly sprang from several common qualities—a keen power of observation, an equally keen love of mingling with all sorts and conditions of men, and a lifelong habit of mental can-dour. But at the same time in one basic condition they were poles apart. John-son looked at things from the point of view of a Christian, Anatole France from that of a pagan; yet these opposite points of view produced in both men a similar result—a permanent sense of emotional and intellectual depression. Johnson was perpetually perplexed by hopes and fears of his eternal salvation, and his many Prayers and Meditations which have been preserved are lifelong evidence of it:

"I rose according to my resolution, and am now to begin another year (January 1781), I hope with an amendment of life. I will not despair. Help me, help me, O my God ".

France, on the other hand, found so much pleasure in existence that he was never resigned to the shortness of human life.

# JOHNSON & WORDSWORTH
# IN THE HIGHLANDS

SAINTE-BEUVE, in his famous *Portraits
Littéraires*, brings together two French
poets, Régnier and Chénier, as admirable types of their respective schools of
poetry. It suggests a comparison between
the mental attitudes of Johnson and
Wordsworth in the Highlands. Johnson
made his tour to the Hebrides in 1773;
Wordsworth went to Scotland thirty
years later. They visited many of the same
towns and many of the same natural
objects; and between the day on which
Johnson departed from London to meet
Boswell in Edinburgh, and the day
on which Wordsworth, with his sister
Dorothy and Coleridge, left Keswick,
there had been little change in the general
condition of the Highlands. There were
few inns to be found and, as we to-day
understand the word, no hotels at all;
public accommodation was intolerably

bad, a traveller being often obliged to be satisfied with a night's lodging in a miserable hovel. Such was the ferryman's hut on the edge of Loch Katrine. Wordsworth and Coleridge had to sleep in an adjacent barn on the hay, while Dorothy Wordsworth made the best of a bed of chaff in the cottage. The party drank coffee and ate barley-bread and butter while the smoke came in gusts and spread along the walls above their heads into the chimney where the hens were roosting. At Glen Elg Johnson and Boswell were shown "into a room damp and dirty, with bare walls, a variety of bad smells, a coarse black greasy fir table and forms of the same kind". The two travellers had to send for hay, on which Johnson reposed, enveloped in his overcoat.

Johnson, in chronic ill health, resolutely setting forth to visit the Western Islands, to travel over mountain passes and on bad roads through stony glens, to navigate in a small craft a stormy and treacherous sea, will always hold our

admiration for uncommon and coura-
geous energy. For courage was indeed
required in anyone who, in the eighteenth
century, would visit the Western Islands.
When one reads Boswell's story of the
return from Skye to the Island of Mull,
how the little coaster ran for shelter to
the Island of Col in the darkening night
in a fierce storm of wind and rain, and
how Johnson lay below apparently cheer-
ful and undisturbed, one can better appreciate his pluck.

Wordsworth, under the existing conditions of Highland travel, had many advantages over Johnson, who was sixty-
four, with a sedentary, valetudinarian
life behind him, a man whose ordinary
exercise had been a walk down Fleet
Street or a stroll with Mrs Thrale in her
garden at Streatham. Wordsworth and his
sister, on the other hand, were still young,
accustomed to a simple, open-air life on
the Westmorland hillsides.

If the contrast between the disposi-
tions and the habits of the tourists was

remarkable, their appearance on their travels was also noteworthy. Johnson, from necessity, was from time to time obliged to ride and was even more uncomfortable on horseback than was Wordsworth as a driver. Johnson's great body, enveloped in a heavy brown coat, swayed backwards and forwards as he brandished his large oak stick and laughed at the gillie who, as he led the horse, tried to amuse the rider by his shrill whistling. Wordsworth, an excellent walker, but a bad driver, drove an animal which had a partiality for backing up steep banks or sidling into the parapets of bridges, while the poet sat in an old one-horse vehicle, dressed in a suit of russet brown, with a broad flapping straw hat to protect his weak eyes.

Johnson and Wordsworth not only differed markedly in character and in mental outlook, but went to the Highlands in quite opposite frames of mind. Johnson was primarily an intelligent traveller, who was determined, as Boswell says, to see as much of Scotland as he could during August and September. He was interested mainly in the country as it affected the inhabitants, for he thought that in the Hebrides he "might contemplate a system of life almost totally different from what he had been accustomed to see". "I have now", he wrote to Mrs Thrale from Skye, "the pleasure of going where nobody goes, and seeing what nobody sees". Johnson desired to observe the Scotch at home in a distant and almost inaccessible region. "In a foreign country", wrote Gibbon, "curiosity is our business and our pleasure". Curiosity, in the widest sense, was certainly a pleasure to Johnson, and to him, as to his contemporaries, Scotland was a foreign country. Wordsworth, on the contrary, started for the North with no inquisitive eye, with no determination to acquire positive knowledge. He has told us himself his simple object in the lines in which he bade farewell to his home, and which, though not of the best, are autobiographically interesting. He went

> To cull contentment upon wildest shores
> And luxuries extract from bleakest moors.

Johnson, the essayist, and Wordsworth, the poet, may thus be said to represent two different classes, the merely intelligent and the reflective. From the point of view of travel the two types are irreconcilable, for they regard scenery from different points of view. Wordsworth certainly neither desired nor needed grand or beautiful scenery; the suggestions of a scene, however homely, permeated his mentality. When his eye perceived a sea loch—Loch Long or Loch Fyne—winding among the mountains, his mind penetrated the hillside and the water lapping the rocky brink—

> And with the coming of the tide,
> Come boats and ships that safely ride
> Between the woods and lofty rocks;
> And to the shepherds with their flocks
>    Bring tales of distant lands.

Thoughts like these never arose in Johnson's unimaginative mind; he regarded material objects as remarkable phenomena, and he looked at everything from this point of view. They did not arouse his emotion. The scenery of the Highlands was, in fact, repulsive to Johnson. On the way from Fort Augustus to the coast the party halted for an hour at noon on a fine day in a glen which Johnson grudgingly describes as "sufficiently verdant". It does not take much imagination to realize how delightful it must have been—the varying lights, the soft air, the stillness broken only by the ripple of the burn. But Johnson found no pleasure in the place. "Before me", he wrote in his journal, "were high hills which by hindering the eye from ranging forced the mind to find entertainment for itself". The remainder of this portion of the *Journey* is in the same vein—the best that can be said for the locality was that there were worse places to be found.

In Hardy's *Return of the Native* most of the action of the story occurs on or near a barren tract of land which he calls Egdon Heath; but the waste is endowed with vitality: "The place"—night is approaching—"became full of watchful intentness. Now, when other things sank brooding to sleep, the heath appeared slowly to awake and listen". Single passages of a continuous description cannot do justice to it, but Hardy's pictures of Egdon Heath show how far we have gone in appreciation of scenery since Johnson sat musing by the burn near Glenshiel. Johnson did not make the smallest effort to penetrate as Wordsworth penetrated, sometimes perhaps too painfully, into the heart of a natural object, however small; he was not concerned to discover the relation of a daffodil or a daisy to human life. Mountains, lakes and trees passed before his eyes and were forgotten; the poet, on the other hand, retained scenes, and individuals identified with them, in his mind till, after long germinating, his thought bore fruit in the form of expressed reflections. For Wordsworth the tour, from first to last, was constantly touching emotional chords. No object was too insignificant to be remembered, and we see the result in many poems, as in *The Highland Girl* and in *Rob Roy's Grave*.

Johnson was also impelled to verse, but he wrote Horatian odes on Skye and on Mrs Thrale. No personality could be more opposite to the wild western Highlands than the mistress of what Boswell called the "elegant villa" at Streatham with its comfortable culture; and the very fact that Johnson spent an evening in Skye composing a Latin ode to the lady whom he designates "Thralia dulcis" shows that his heart was not in the Highlands, but in London. From the beginning to the end of the tour he never got, or tried to get, below the surface of things, and had no perception of the suggestions of nature. He could never have felt the pathos of the simple scene which Wordsworth has embodied in *The Highland Girl*.

One may see the differences of personal temperament very vividly by following the travellers over one route, and noting the contrast in their impressions. Johnson and Boswell, on their return from the Western Islands, landed at Oban, and rode to Inverary; from there they went round the head of Loch Fyne and over the lonely Pass of Glencroe. This pass debouches on to Loch Long, and, following its shores, the travellers went round its head to Arrochar and then across the neck of land which separates the sea loch from Loch Lomond at Tarbet. Next, skirting the lower part of this loch, they reached Dumbarton and its rock. Anyone may take the same route to-day and have no difficulty whatever, so little is changed, in appreciating Johnson's ride. Wordsworth and his sister journeyed in an opposite direction, but went no further west than Inverary, when they turned inland to Loch Awe. Johnson probably enjoyed himself most at Inverary. Why? Because he was made much of by the hospitable Duke of Argyll, by whom he was entertained to dinner at the castle, where he enjoyed the sociability of the evening. One expression is characteristic. Speaking of the castle, he said, "What I admire here is the total defiance of expense". Not a word about sunset or sunrise, about lights or shades on mountain sides. Presently he approached the charming scenery of Loch Lomond with its wooded islands clustered on its lower reaches; of these he says in his *Journey*: "Had Loch Lomond been in a happier climate it would have been the boast of wealth and vanity to own one of the little spots which it encloses, and to have employed upon it all the arts of embellishment". Need we be surprised, after this, that Johnson, as he quitted the house near Dumbarton of Commissary Smollett, remarked with obvious delight, "We have had more solid talk here than at any place where we have been"? This is the expression of the lettered, the urban, the sociable man who does not enjoy nature; for him nature is a sealed book and he rejoices to be again in the company of clever men.

Yet we need not scorn Johnson's incapacity to understand the aesthetic value of the Highlands; for in his age the appreciation of nature, as we know it, scarcely existed. "Gloomy hills assailed by the winter tempest, lakes concealed in blue mist and cold lonely heaths", is Gibbon's idea of Scotland. After all, the Highlands are bleak and barren. One of the most inhospitable tracts is the Moor of Ranoch, which nevertheless can, in changes of light and shade, give to some no little pleasure. But even to-day those who can appreciate the charm of the Highlands are in a minority; among the mountains and glens most people obtain their enjoyment from sport or physical exercise, while the interest of others is mainly excited by a difference in the landscape from that in which they habitually live. Few possess what Bage-

hot called the mystical sense which "finds
a motion in the mountain and a power in
the waves and a meaning in the long
white line of the shore and a thought in
the blue of heaven". Johnson certainly
did not, and we understand him better
when we realize the negative, as well as
the positive, side of his character.

Wordsworth, on the other hand, with
trained and sympathetic eye, found in
every yard of the same journey some new
and suggestive picture. He and his sister
approach the bleak summit of the Pass of
Glencroe. "The sun had set before we
had dismounted from the car to walk up
the steep hill at the end of the glen.
Clouds were heavy all over the sky.
Some of a brilliant yellow hue shed a
light like bright moonlight upon the
mountains". At the summit is a stone
seat with the inscription, "Rest and be
thankful". Johnson, when he saw it,
would most likely make some incisive
remark to Boswell such as, "Sir, this is
a foolish inscription; a traveller should

not rest and be thankful till he reaches his journey's end". As it was, in his *Journey* he merely quotes the inscription and says of Glencroe that it is a bleak and dreary region. Yet this is the pass which Dorothy Wordsworth describes so delightfully, and which fixed itself in Wordsworth's brooding memory. Among the poems which have been ascribed to a tour in Scotland, many years later, in 1831, is one entitled *Rest and be thankful at the Head of Glencroe*:

Doubling and doubling with laborious walk,
Who, that has gained at length the wished for
    height,
This brief, this simple wayside call can slight,
And rest not thankful? Whether cheered by
    talk
With some loved friend or by the unseen hawk
Whistling to clouds and skyborn streams that
    shine
At the sun's outbreak as with light divine.

These lines probably embody impressions absorbed on that beautiful autumn evening which Dorothy Wordsworth depicts as she and her brother attained the highest point of the glen, rather than the thoughts of later years.[1] Presumably they would leave the stone and move along the level bit of road which is the beginning of the descent to Glen King-lass, and then

We saw the western sky a glorious mass of clouds uprising from a sea of distant mountains, stretched out in length before us towards the west, and close by us was a small lake or tarn. From the reflection of the crimson clouds the water appeared of a deep red, like melted rubies, yet with a mixture of grey or blackish hue; the gorgeous light of the sky, with the singular colour of the lake made the scene exceedingly romantic.

Wordsworth and his sister so resembled each other in mind and temperament that one feels that she describes as much his, as her, impressions of the evening in these mountain solitudes. It is true that

[1] Wordsworth does not himself state when he wrote these lines. I have some doubt whether he and his daughter went to Glencroe in 1831. It is said in Knight's *Life* that they returned from Mull to Killin, Glencroe and Loch Lomond. Glencroe is not in the route from Killin to Loch Lomond.

Johnson crossed the pass in wind and rain, and that the Wordsworths saw it in fine weather, but it will be remembered that when Johnson rested, in a sunny noontide, near Glen Elg, the scenery around him was no more attractive than was the summit of Glencroe on a wild autumn day. For Johnson it was a "bleak and dreary region" and there was an end on't.

# §III

## JOHNSON OUT OF TOWN

*The Trip to Harwich*
*In the Country*

# THE TRIP TO HARWICH

THE journey of Johnson and Boswell to
Harwich in 1763 is usually regarded only
as an isolated episode in their friendship;
it has, however, a larger value and is interesting also from another point of view.
We obtain a picture of a scene in England
in the eighteenth century with these two
famous figures in the foreground. For
Harwich was a busy port, one from
which there was constant communication with Holland, where vessels could
lie quietly at anchor and where passengers could embark and land in reasonable
comfort.

Coming to our two travellers, the incidents of the trip should be recalled. It
was on Friday, 4 August 1763, that Johnson and Boswell left London by coach
for Harwich, Boswell being bound for
Utrecht to study law. On their journey

they stayed for a night at Colchester, and on 5 August, hot and dusty after a morning's drive of twenty-one miles, reached Harwich at noon, in time for a midday dinner. They would, no doubt, alight at the Three Cups in Church Street, then and for many years after the principal inn of this seaport. When they had finished this midday dinner, which perhaps was served in the room in which, at the end of the century, Nelson used to dine, the Doctor and his young friend walked to the church which is hard by, at the top of the street. Here, strange as it may seem to most people, Johnson made Boswell kneel at the altar, telling him that as he was about to leave his native country he should recommend himself to the protection of his Creator and Redeemer. This was a natural act on Johnson's part, for, unlike most men, he carried his religion into his daily life. The prayer that his work might be productive of good, which he wrote before he issued the *Rambler*, is famous, and now at Harwich, whether willing or not, Boswell must follow his example. From the church the Doctor and Boswell walked down Church Street to the beach, beyond which in the quiet waters of the Stour the vessel lay at anchor which was to carry the young Scotsman across the North Sea.

To-day the scene can easily be realized. If the steamboat piers were removed one would see the streets of the little town ending on a sloping beach in the estuary of the Stour; to the right, then as now, round the point was a broad expanse of water which led to the open sea. The packet would lie at high water close to the land ready to sail, and boatmen would carry passengers to her in their small boats. As the vessel got under weigh Johnson stood watching its departure. "I kept my eyes upon him", writes Boswell in his inimitable way, "for a considerable time, while he remained rolling his majestic frame in his usual manner, and at last I perceived him walk back into the town and he disappeared". Boswell, as he told him, had feared that if the Doctor's return to London were delayed it would be "terrible" to be detained in so dull a place. But the only reply he received was a characteristic reproof—"Don't, sir, accustom yourself to use big words for little matters".

After the packet had sailed Boswell disappears from the scene, but without his narrative one may well imagine Johnson hurrying in his lumbering way, "rolling his majestic frame", up Church Street, and then stopping out of breath on The Green, whence he would have an uninterrupted view of the estuary and could watch the sails of the packet disappear down the broad channel to the North Sea, as one may to-day see the steamers passing to Belgium and Holland. Then the Doctor had but to return to the inn and leave Harwich by the afternoon coach.

The popular idea of Johnson is of a Londoner who found London the only place worth living in. This mythical Johnson has been created not a little from sayings of his own, such as "a man who is tired of London is tired of life", and "the full tide of human existence is at Charing Cross". But no one was more keen to visit other localities or more desirous of personal knowledge of peoples and places. In 1777, apropos of the Hebridean expedition, he said to Boswell: "In the meantime it may not be amiss to contrive some other little adventure", and, when he wrote to tell Boswell that the *Journey to the Hebrides* was on the eve of publication, he concluded by asking, "Shall we touch the Continent?" He was, at the moment, already thinking of another tour, and when Boswell was, in 1763, considering a visit to Holland, "Johnson", he says, "advises me in general to move about a good deal"— the advice of a born traveller. The short visit to Harwich is further evidence of this spirit of adventure.

The truth is that Johnson had all the

instincts of a traveller—curiosity, hardi-
hood, courage and patience, more so
than any other man of letters of his time.
No better evidence of this can be found
than the statement of Mrs Thrale, who
so well understood her old friend.

"His desire", she says, "to go abroad, par-
ticularly to see Italy, was very great.... He
loved indeed the very act of travelling, and I
cannot tell how far one might have taken him
in a carriage before he would have wished for
refreshment. He was therefore in some respects an admirable companion on the road, as he
piqued himself upon feeling no inconvenience,
and on despising no accommodations. On the
other hand however, he expected no one else
to feel any, and felt exceedingly inflamed with
anger if anyone complained of the rain, the sun,
or the dust".

Before this Harwich expedition the Doctor had visited Oxford, once in July
1754, when he remained for purposes of
literary research for five weeks, and again
after the death of his mother in 1759.
This time he went merely, as far as one
can judge, for the sake of the trip. Then

in 1762 he joined Sir Joshua Reynolds in
an expedition, as it may well be called, to
Plymouth. Sir Joshua had a good reason
for making this long and fatiguing
journey; he was going to his homeland.
But obviously it was love of travel which
caused Johnson to accompany Reynolds,
that and nothing more. Unfortunately
for us this journey occurred before Johnson and Boswell met, and only a few details of it have been preserved. I have
examined the diaries of Sir Joshua which
are preserved in the Library of the Royal
Academy; they contain, however, only
bare entries of dates and places, nothing
whatever of a personal nature, but they
confirm the fact that the travellers left
London on 16 August and arrived back
on 26 September. Still, their perusal makes
the journey now more vivid and lifelike,
enabling us to visualize the movements
of the two friends, though it adds nothing
to our knowledge of this trip. For our
particular and present purpose, this is
immaterial; it is the mere fact of the long

journey to and from the West which shows how Johnson enjoyed travel. It is worth while also to recall the visit to old Mr Langton—Bennet Langton's father —in Lincolnshire in 1764. At his house was a good library and pleasant company, but the journey was nevertheless a considerable one for a Londoner of sedentary habits. Again, in August of the same year the Doctor paid a visit to Dr Percy in Northamptonshire, making a second long journey in one year. The trip to Harwich is more interesting and suggestive than any of these, because on this occasion Boswell was Johnson's companion. The day and a half which they spent on their way illustrates very well Mrs Thrale's description of Johnson as a traveller, "that he piqued himself on feeling no inconvenience", for, so far from being bored by the confinement of the coach, he obviously enjoyed his talk and jokes with the woman who was one of the company and his discussions with the young Dutchman on the criminal law

of Holland. One is so accustomed to
think of the Doctor at the Turk's Head
or at Streatham living a sedentary life,
that it is difficult to imagine him in a
coach, jolting through the eastern counties and talking with his fellow-pas-
sengers. When one does, then one begins to appreciate Johnson the traveller,
unfamiliar though in this form he is to
most of us.

At any rate, it seems clear that Johnson
would hardly have accompanied Boswell
to Harwich from personal affection only,
for they first met on 16 May of the same
year. The famous friendship was, therefore, but three months old. Another
thing to bear in mind is that Johnson was
constantly in a state of physical suffering,
and one does not, unless in robust health,
undergo fatigue such as that of a trip in
a stage-coach to Harwich and back, short
as it might be considered, unless stimulated by some strong desire. The desire
in Johnson was to visit a seaport which
in his day was an important place of de-

parture to, and arrival from, the Continent, and also to see another bit of England. A spirit of adventure, and a thirst for knowledge which was not limited to the reading of books were causes of the journey to Harwich, illustrating vividly traits in Johnson's character which are often overlooked.

Another reason for the journey to Harwich has been suggested. Lord Rosebery, in his address on Johnson, delivered in 1909, said, "there was much of the paternal in his relation to his biographer", and again, "he came to love Boswell". These two feelings, in Lord Rosebery's opinion, were the causes of the trip to the Essex seaport. But paternal feeling, however strong, could not have been enough of itself to induce Johnson to incur the expense and trouble of a journey to Harwich and back to London in the dust of August, for Boswell was twenty-two years of age, and did not require the attention of a parent on a journey, and affection has not much opportunity of expression either in a stage-coach or at an inn. Actual love of travel in the largest sense, in the first place, and the opportunity of taking the journey with an already appreciated companion were clearly the causes of this expedition, rather than some kind of paternal feeling or mere "love of Boswell". This trip to Harwich is therefore memorable, partly because it was indicative of the travelling instinct in Johnson and partly because it was, as regards companionship with Boswell, in a sense experimental. In consequence of its success it was the humble precursor of and a precedent for the Doctor's famous journey to the Hebrides exactly ten years later with the same companion.

In this visit to Harwich he found the young Boswell an agreeable companion, "whose gaiety of conversation and civility of manners", as he wrote on the first page of the *Journey*, "are sufficient to counteract the inconveniences of travel". May it not therefore be said, with some confidence, that but for this short trip to Harwich, on which Johnson tested Boswell as a travelling companion, there would perhaps have been no prolonged journey to the Western Isles?

# IN THE COUNTRY

On a fine day in July 1763 Johnson and Boswell took a boat down the Thames to Greenwich. One would like to have seen them, but at least we can imagine them sitting in the stern talking and arguing and sometimes chatting with the boatman. In the evening they took a walk in Greenwich Park, in the course of which Johnson said to his companion: "Is not this very fine?" But Boswell having, as he candidly admits, "no exquisite relish for the beauties of Nature, and being more delighted with 'the busy hum of men'", replied: "Yes, sir, but not equal to Fleet Street". To this the Doctor answered: "You are quite right, sir". This reply, and other similar remarks of Johnson's in praise of London and of town life which are to be found in Boswell's book, have left an impression in many minds that Johnson disliked the country. One thing, however, is clear, that for a man with his literary occupations he spent an unusual amount of time in the country in an age when a visit to Bath or Tunbridge Wells was almost the only form of semi-rural recreation for those who could afford to stay, for a short time, out of London. Johnson's attitude towards the country, it must be at once conceded, was that of a temporary dweller in it; he went there willingly enough and for sound reasons, but not for love of it. He had no wish to remain in it permanently, and he obtained no aesthetic pleasure from it. To a man whose chief enjoyment in life was social intercourse—either with men who, like Thurlow and Burke, would put their wits against his and so produce interchange of thought, who would amuse him, as Goldsmith and Fanny Burney did, or who would listen appreciatively to the opinions which he enunciated—the country was deficient in many of the things which to him made life worth living. This is what the Doctor meant when he contemptuously said: "They who are content to live in the country are fit for the country". He himself was not only temperamentally unfit, but was there without an occupation. On another occasion this statement was amplified, for he told Boswell that "no wise man will go to live in the country unless he has something to do which will be better done in the country". It was for this reason that, while he thought the country unsuitable for men like himself, he considered that the man of property should remain at home for he had "something to do", and he "ought to consider himself as having the charge of a district over which he is to diffuse civility and happiness", which last words in modern language may be translated as hospitality and social work. Johnson, on the contrary, speaking broadly, had from the nature of his occupations and the character of his pleasures nothing to do out of London.

R                                        9

But he would allow the country gentleman one exception to the rule that he should remain at home: "A country gentleman", he said, "should bring his lady to visit London as soon as he can, that they may have agreeable topics for conversation when they are by themselves". Johnson's memories of London would, no doubt, have furnished topics for conversation for an indefinite time, but those which interested the Squire Westerns of the countryside, if they interested them at all, would very soon come to an end. Johnson's opinion of the country seems, in fact, to be accurately summarized in one sentence in the *Rambler* in a paper on pastoral poetry. "In childhood", he says, "we turn our thoughts to the country, as to the region of pleasure, we recur to it in old age as a port of rest". To anyone, in fact, except a boy or a sexagenarian, the country was inferior to the town.

For forming these views the Doctor had sufficient opportunities, for his visits

to the country were sometimes lengthy.
He stayed, for instance, in 1777 from
August to the beginning of October at
Ashbourne with Dr Taylor, parson and
squire, but more squire than parson, of
whom Boswell's description is that "his
size and figure and countenance and
manners were those of a hearty English
squire". Taylor's was a purely country
home, and he was famous in his county
as a breeder of cattle; in these animals Dr
Johnson appears to have been interested,
surprising though it may seem to us,
until we recollect that he found instruction or amusement in everything which
came his way. This fortunate circum-
stance enabled him for a time to stay,
without repining, in the country.

When we accompany Johnson to the
country we are struck by some de-
ficiencies in Boswell's *Life*. We do not
know how Johnson passed his time as,
for instance, at Ashbourne, although
Boswell himself was there during this
visit from 14 to 24 September; he chro-

nicles what his hero says and not what he does. In the open air Johnson could be remarkably active considering his physical defects. He was no sportsman, his sight would never have allowed him to fire a gun with effect or with safety to others. Nor was he a horseman, though Mrs Thrale tells us that when at Brighton he rode Mr Thrale's old hunter and compassed fifty miles in a day without fatigue. One may doubt whether the old hunter would not have found five miles enough with Johnson on his back, and no harriers at Brighton or anywhere else ever ran fifty miles in a day. For gardening and horticulture the Doctor had no taste. To drive, the faster the better, in a coach gave him pleasure, but in the eighteenth century the lanes of Derbyshire were unsuited to this recreation, and we must conclude that walking in the pleasure grounds of the house in which he was a guest was his main out-of-door amusement, if such it could be called. We know that when he visited Lichfield, as

he did in 1775, from 10 June to the beginning of August—"I am returned",
he wrote to Boswell, on the 27th, "from
the annual ramble into the middle counties"—and again in the following year,
he walked daily to Stowhill, a pleasant
stroll of some fifteen minutes through
the meadows from the town. Boswell
was his companion during the visit in
1776, and tells us that two sisters, Mrs
Aston and Mrs Gastrel, friends of the
Doctor, lived on this "gentle eminence,
each owning", as he says, "a house, a
garden, and a pleasure ground". These
can still be seen, Stow House where
Mrs Aston lived, and "the lower house",
once the home of Mrs Gastrel.

Though Johnson disliked exercise,
when there was an object in view, especially pleasant conversation, he was
willing to walk. With the knowledge
that we have of the two visits to Lichfield, then a purely country town, we
may conclude that both in Lincolnshire
with the Langtons, and at Ashbourne

with Taylor, some part of Johnson's time was occupied in walking. But there is a monotony in this exercise which would not be agreeable to him; and as he had no other resource except to sit in the house but without a company of friends, it is not surprising that by the end of September both Taylor and himself were pleased when the visit in 1777 was approaching its end. Johnson, though he often bemoaned his own idleness, was in fact a strenuous worker; and it must have been trying for Doctor Taylor to be criticized as a divine, even though Johnson characteristically passed some part of his time in writing sermons for his bucolic friend.

In the summer of 1774 Johnson went for a tour in Wales with the Thrales, staying, as was necessary, at various places in England on the outward and on the return journey. The party left Streatham on 5 July, and were back in London by 30 September. Thus Johnson spent nearly three months out of London.

From these and other visits, such as that in August 1765 to Dr Percy at Easton Neston in Northamptonshire, omitting altogether the journey to the Hebrides, which was in the nature of travel in an unknown land and quite an abnormal feat, we can form a definite idea of Johnson's attitude to the country.

One must differentiate between country life—the people, their work and their pleasures—and the country: that is, nature, as it was called in the eighteenth century, inanimate objects. Human life invariably teemed with interest for the Doctor, he enjoyed it, was amused by it, and was vexed by it. Lady Bustle, in the *Rambler*, of whom he makes fun for her absorption in cooking and jams and for her want of ideas outside of her domestic employment, is a sketch from life, either from actual sight or from accurate description. But neither this good lady nor other figures who move through the pages of Johnson's two periodicals could have been produced by a mere student, a compiler of dictionaries only. They were drawn by a man of the world who, in spite of his attachment to Fleet Street, found much to instruct and amuse him in a country village.

Partly from weak sight, but more from his objective temperament, he cared nothing about natural objects, and except in some special instance they neither gave him pleasure nor produced any mental impression. Mrs Thrale, who was inclined to take literally many of Johnson's statements, which he intended as pleasantries, after saying that Johnson hated to hear about prospects and views, goes on to tell us that he loved the sight of fine forest trees, but detested Brighthelmstone downs, "because it was a country so truly desolate", he said, "that if one had a mind to hang oneself for desperation at being obliged to live there, it would be difficult to find a tree on which to fasten the rope". This extract is enlightening. Fine forest trees are exactly the objects to strike an intelligent observer, but the outspreading and haunting downs are silent spaces which would at once depress the lover of the town and would probably diminish his intellectual vitality. The same kind of approach towards natural objects can constantly be seen in Johnson's diary of the Welsh tour. Of the River Dove—the party had not yet reached Wales—he notes that "the river is small, the rocks are grand". Only the size of the things he sees in this Derbyshire vale is noticeable. "In one place", he continues, "where the rocks approached, I proposed to build an arch from rock to rock over the stream with a summer house upon it. The water murmured pleasantly among the stones". Here there is no appreciation of the scenery, which only suggests to him an ingenious mode of altering it by the addition of a building. Sometimes, too, he showed himself to have little sense of proportion. Of Hawkstone in Shropshire—an imposing hill, it may be admitted, rising as it does out of a fertile and level district—he says that it is "a region abounding with striking scenes and terrific grandeur". Johnson once told Boswell not to use big words for small things, but here he falls into the fault himself, without in any way representing the scene before him.

In conversation Johnson always liked to be emphatic and striking; it became a habit and it sometimes resulted in an over-emphasis which does not bear critical examination. His written opinions therefore are often more valuable than his sayings in company, and when we come to read his statements about the country we find the plain common-sense view which we should expect. "Novelty itself is a source of gratification; and Milton justly observes, that to him who has been long pent up in cities, no rural object can be presented which will not delight or refresh some of his senses." In this passage Johnson recognizes the value of change of scene and the contrast

between country and town, not perhaps
an enthusiastic way of regarding the
country, though it was one which he obviously carried into practice. In another
passage, also to be found in one of the
*Rambler* papers, he says, "the freshness
of the air, the verdure of the woods, the
paint of the meadows, and the unex-
hausted variety which summer scatters
upon the earth, may easily give delight
to an unlearned observer". This is more
appreciative, but the last phrase suggests
that he himself would not, except from
a purely material point of view, obtain
appreciable advantage from rural scenes.

When Johnson writes about the spring
he mentions flowers and fields, but they
suggest only a moral lesson. The gaiety
of the scene gives pleasure, but "there
are men who hurry away from all the
varieties of rural beauty to use their hours
and divert their thoughts by cards, or
assemblies, a tavern dinner, or the prattle
of the day". Johnson depicts himself
when, in the same number, he writes: "A

man that has formed this habit of turning every new object to his entertainment, finds in the production of nature an inexhaustible stock of materials upon which he can employ himself without any temptation or malevolence". To watch hay-makers in the meadows afforded to a man like Johnson what he called "entertainment", and it was, he considered, better for inferior beings to stroll through the fields on a sunny afternoon than to hasten back to town merely to listen to the idle "prattle of the day". But when Henry Thrale, who seems to have had some appreciation of scenery, desired to point out features of a landscape, he only elicited from the Doctor a brusque reply which summarizes Johnson's intellectual position on this subject: "A blade of grass is always a blade of grass, whether in one country or another; let us if we do talk, talk about something; men and women are my subjects of inquiry; let us see how these differ from those we have left behind".

It is worth while to contrast this general attitude of Johnson with that of his contemporary, Gray. They did not appreciate each other. Johnson thought Gray dull, and Gray disliked Johnson's frequently dictatorial manner. Gray loved to ramble about the country; he was drawn into it and absorbed it. In 1770 he enjoyed a six weeks' ramble through Worcestershire and the adjoining counties—"the very light and principal feature in my journey", he wrote to his friend, Thomas Wharton, "was the River Wye; its banks", he continues, "are a succession of nameless wonders"; the vale of Monmouth, he said, was the delight of his eyes; and in his diary of a ramble in the Lake Country in the previous year we find an exquisitely perceptive and sensitive description of an evening among the hills. "In the evening walk'd alone down to the Lake by the side of Crow Park after sunset and saw the solemn colouring of night draw on, the last gleam of sunshine fading away on the hill-tops, the deep serene of the waters, and the long shadows of the mountains thrown across them, till they nearly touched the hithermost shore; at distance heard the murmur of many waterfalls, not audible in the daytime; wished for the moon, but she was *dark to me and silent, hid in her vacant interlunar cave.*"

Nothing can better make us realize Johnson's emotional barrenness amidst the sights and sounds of the country than these extracts from the diary of another man of letters of Johnson's own period. Gray, it may be admitted, was aesthetically in advance of his time, and was endowed with a most sensitive temperament, while Johnson was essentially representative of his age, and had a mind insensible to natural beauty. Therefore, when we accompany Johnson into the country, we must accept his want of emotional reaction at the sight of natural objects; his obvious aesthetic limitations arising not only from temperament, but also from the character of the age in which he lived. Yet we understand him better, and these defects—and no one is perfect—do not lessen our affection and respect for Samuel Johnson.

# INDEX

For EU product safety concerns, contact us at Calle de José Abascal, 56–1°,
28003 Madrid, Spain or eugpsr@cambridge.org.

www.ingramcontent.com/pod-product-compliance
Ingram Content Group UK Ltd.
Pitfield, Milton Keynes, MK11 3LW, UK
UKHW012332130625
459647UK00009B/235